Yorkshire
Record
BREAKERS

The ultimate compendium
of when Yorkshire did it best!

feats, facts
and fabulous firsts

Written and compiled by
Adrian Braddy

Dalesman

Published in Great Britain in 2017 by Dalesman
an imprint of
Country Publications Ltd
The Water Mill, Broughton Hall, Skipton BD23 3AG
www.dalesman.co.uk

ISBN: 978-1-85568-366-2

Printed in China by 1010 Printing International Ltd

Introduction

Yorkshire is a county of record breakers. It has been the birthplace of the nation's tallest, shortest, heaviest and oldest people. Within its broad acres you can find the world's oldest working railway, football club and theatre. This is the county that brought the world manned flight, moving pictures and stainless steel. And it is home to the oldest sweet shop, pub, chemist shop and horse race.

Yorkshire also holds the records for the largest piece of fossilised human excrement ever found, the biggest ball of cling film ever wrapped and the world's longest group hug. And it goes without saying that the county has produced the globe's biggest portion of fish and chips, the largest pie and the most colossal Yorkshire pud.

We have brought together all these and many more in what we hope is the most comprehensive collection of Yorkshire records, firsts and feats ever published. Both "official" and "unofficial" records are included, as are records set in Yorkshire that have since been broken. There are records both triumphant and trivial, records that will make you smile and others that will make you proud.

And if there's a record that doesn't feature in these pages, why not go out and break it, so we can include it in the second edition?

Adrian Braddy

Britain's tallest ever man

William Bradley

William Bradley, better known as Giant Bradley, measured a remarkable 7ft 9in (2.36m), making him the tallest recorded British man in history.

Born in Market Weighton, in the East Riding of Yorkshire, in 1787, his parents were both of average height. His dad, a master tailor, was 5ft 9in (1.75m).

Bradley began touring Britain with a "freak show" under the alias of the Yorkshire Giant, along with an immense hog, the Yorkshire Pig. By 1815 he had chosen to work independently and would charge a shilling apiece for people to visit him in rooms he hired as he toured the country. He was even presented before King George III at Windsor. The King gave him a gold watch on a chain, which he treasured for the rest of his life.

Bradley died aged thirty-three in his home town. The main road which passes through Market Weighton is named Giant Bradley Way in his honour and Giant Bradley Day takes place in the town every May.

Born in 1853, Henry Alexander Cooper, of Norton, near Malton, North Yorkshire, came close to beating Bradley's record. He grew to 7ft 6in (2.28m). His hands were 13in (33cm) long and his feet measured 17in (43cm) in length.

William Bradley at
18 years of age

5

World's smallest man

Edwin Calvert

General Tom Thumb achieved worldwide fame in the 1800s as he toured America and Europe with circus pioneer PT Barnum. Real name Charles Stratton, the American was born with dwarfism and was considered the smallest man in the world. He was aged just five when he first began touring, though Barnum claimed he was in fact eleven. Regularly performing before European royalty, Tom Thumb continued to grow until he reached his maximum height of 3ft 3in (99cm), aged twenty-one.

At this time, in Skipton, North Yorkshire, lived Edwin Calvert. Four years Stratton's junior, the young Yorkshireman believed he was smaller than General Tom Thumb. As a result he was known by friends as the Commander-in-chief – thereby outranking the General.

The two dwarfs met while Stratton was on a tour of Britain and they swapped clothes to assess which was truly the smallest. It seemed the Commander-in-chief was indeed some 3in shorter than the General. A book of the time reported: "Tom Thumb took off his own boots, and the other got into them; he could then easily throw them off, as they were too large for him."

Fame beckoned. "Arrangements were being made for him to be presented to the Queen; a court dress was being made; and in less than a month he was going to London and then on the Continent for exhibition."

Sadly, the tour never happened, as Calvert died, just a few months after meeting Tom Thumb, on 7th August 1859.

His tombstone can still be found in Skipton. It stands against the wall of Christ Church, with an inscription that reads: "In memory of Edwin Calvert, known by the title of the Commander-in-chief, being the smallest and most perfect man in the world, being under 36 inches in height and weighing 23 and one-half pounds."

England's heaviest man

Joseph Coltman (1776–1837), incumbent curate of Beverley Minster for twenty-four years, was said to be the heaviest man then living in England. He weighed thirty-seven stone and eight pounds (238.5kg).

Rev Coltman in silhouette on his custom-made bike

Britain's tallest twins

In the early 1980s, Jonathan and Mark Carratt, of Maltby, South Yorkshire, held the record for being the tallest twins in Britain. They measured 6ft 8in (2.03m) and 6ft 9in (2.06m) respectively.

Oldest Englishman of all time (unofficial)

Henry Jenkins, aged 169

Although modern science may dispute the claim, Yorkshire-born Henry Jenkins was said to be the oldest Englishman of all time. Jenkins, who it was claimed lived to the remarkable age of approximately 169, died in 1670 at Ellerton upon Swale, Scorton, North Yorkshire. The supercentenarian claimed to have been born in 1501, though parish registers were not a legal requirement until 1538. He said he was a butler to Lord Conyers of Hornby Castle, later becoming a fisherman. Accounts of the time said he "frequently swam in the rivers after the age of 100 years".

The supercentenarian claimed to have been born in 1501

Chancery Court records show that he stated on oath he was aged "one hundreth fifty and seaven or theirabouts". When asked which notable battle he remembered, he spoke of Flodden Field in 1513, claiming to have carried arrows to the English archers. His burial is recorded in the register of Bolton-on-Swale as having occurred on 9 December, 1670. A grave carried an inscription which read "he lived to the amazing age of 169 years".

Henry Jenkins.

Aged, 169.

Born in 1501, Reign xvi. of Henry vii. Obit. December 3rd, 1670, xxi. of Charles ii.
Who lived during the Reigns of Henry vii, Henry viii. Edward vi,
Queen Mary and Elizabeth,
James i, Charles i, Cromwell, and Charles ii.

Events—Popery the Law of the Land; Remembered the Abbot of Fountain Abbey, Yorkshire, before the dissolution of the Monasteries; Protestant Religion established twice,
Persecution of the Protestants once, also the Government of the Church and State overturned
by Cromwell and his Associates, and Charles i. beheaded January

Oldest British person ever (official)

Charlotte Marion Hughes, aged 115

The claims of the aforementioned Henry Jenkins could not be verified as he was born before records began. The longest-lived person ever officially documented in the UK was Charlotte Marion Hughes of Middlesbrough, North Yorkshire.

She lived under the rule of six monarchs, including Queen Victoria

Born on 1st August 1877, she died on 17th March 1993, aged 115 years, 228 days. She lived under the rule of six monarchs, including Queen Victoria, who was in her fortieth jubilee year when Hughes was born. She also lived through the tenures of twenty-four British Prime Ministers. She enjoyed tea with Margaret Thatcher in 1985 and for her 110th birthday she flew on Concorde to New York.

She lived in her own home in Marske-by-the-Sea, North Yorkshire, until two years before her death, when she moved into a nursing home in nearby Redcar. She remained mentally alert and sharp until the end of her life.

Oldest bride

Winifred Clark became Britain's oldest recorded bride in 1971, when she married at Cantley, South Yorkshire, just one day short of her 100th birthday. Her bridegroom, Albert Smith, was a mere youngster, aged eighty.

World's longest nose and chin

Old Boots of Ripon was a man of unusual appearance. One biography stated: "Among the infinite variety of human countenances that have existed, perhaps none were ever better calculated to excite laughter, mingled with astonishment". Old Boots, who lived in Ripon, West Riding, in the 1700s, had such a long nose and chin that he could hold banknotes between the two.

Old Boots, depicted holding a coin between his nose and chin

World's oldest family

In February 2014 the *Daily Mail* claimed the Brudnells of Middlesbrough, North Yorkshire, could be the "oldest family on the planet". At the time, the eleven siblings ranged in age from sixty-eight to eighty-nine – a combined age of 855 years, beating the official record holders, a family of nine from Italy with a combined age of 828. The siblings, who put their longevity down to "good genes", grew up in a terraced house, sleeping four to a bed.

England's most gargantuan feast

The Cawood Feast

We know how to party in Yorkshire – and one of the biggest of all time was the Great Feast held by George Neville in 1466. He had lately become Archbishop of York and planned a feast to celebrate. He wanted it to be larger than the King's coronation feast and it is said to have lasted four days. With the spread on the Archbishop's table, you can see why.

Right: The Cawood Feast, said to have lasted for four days

He wanted it to be larger than the King's coronation feast and it is said to have lasted four days

On the menu were delights including 608 pikes and breams, 8 seals, 4 porpoises, 104 oxen, 1,000 muttons, 34 porks, 6 wild bulls, 304 veals, 204 kids (goats),

400 swans, 1,000 capons (cockerels), 204 bitterns, 200 pheasants, 400 woodcocks, 100 dozen quails, 200 dozen fowls, 204 cranes, 4,000 pigeons, 2,000 geese, 400 heronshaws, 500 partridges, 100 curlews, 400 plovers, 104 peacocks, 4,000 mallards and teals, 2,000 chickens, 2,000 pigs, 500 stags, does and bucks, 4,000 cold venison pasties, 300 dishes of jellies, 4,000 baked tarts, 3,000 baked custards, 2,000 hot custards, 300 tunne of ale, 100 tunne of wine, 1 pipe of Ypocrass (spiced wine), plus spices, sugared delicates, and wafers plenty.

It was described afterwards as the "greatest feast in all England"

The Cawood Feast, as it became known, is one of history's greatest examples of excess. It was described afterwards as the "greatest feast in all England".

World's biggest gathering of people dressed as Sherlock Holmes

Temple Newsam

A remarkable 443 people donned deerstalkers and brandished pipes and magnifying glasses in an attempt to set an official Guinness World Record at Temple Newsam, West Yorkshire, in 2014. The number of people required to beat the previous record for a gathering of Sherlock Holmes lookalikes was 250, which the event almost doubled. People from around the world joined in the record bid, posing for selfies dressed as the famous detective. All money raised went to the Leeds Teaching Hospitals to help raise funds for the Yorkshire Brain Research Centre. Sadly, although the record was unofficially broken, a supervision error meant it was not officially recognised.

World's oldest working railway

Middleton Railway, Hunslet

Founded in 1758, the Middleton Railway in Hunslet, Leeds, is the world's oldest continuously working public railway. Since 1960 it has been run as a heritage railway by The Middleton Railway Trust. It was the first standard-gauge railway to be taken over and operated by volunteers. In its early days the line was the first to be granted powers by an Act of Parliament and also the first commercial railway to use steam locomotives successfully. In 1812, the steam loco Salamanca ran along the first-ever rack or cog railway – a railway with a toothed rack rail between the running rails.

"The Collier" by Robert Havell (1814), showing a steam locomotive on the Middleton Railway

World's largest railway museum

Although not the largest in terms of floor area (that record is held by La Cité du Train in France), the National Railway Museum in York contains the largest collection of railway objects in the world and attracts the most visitors – more than 900,000 each year.

World's busiest steam heritage line

Carrying 355,000 passengers in 2010, the North Yorkshire Moors Railway is the most-used heritage railway in the UK and it may well be the busiest in the world. The eighteen-mile (29km) railway is the third-longest standard gauge heritage line in the country.

World's largest railway station

Although it no longer holds the title, when it was completed in 1877, York railway station, with its thirteen platforms, was the largest station in the world.

Britain's longest stretch of straight railway track

The longest stretch of straight railway line in Britain, measuring eighteen miles (29km) without a bend, is believed to be the line from the Gilberdyke Junction to a point just east of Selby on the Leeds to Hull Line.

England's highest mainline station

Dent Station, in the West Riding, is the highest mainline station in England at 1,150ft (350m) above sea level.

World's fastest steam locomotive

The LNER Class A4 4468 Mallard (pictured below), built in Doncaster, South Yorkshire, in 1938, beat the world record for a steam locomotive on 3rd July that year when it reached 126mph (203km/h), a record that has never since been bettered.

World's fastest diesel

On 12 June 1973 the prototype InterCity 125 set a world diesel record of 143.2 mph (230.5km/h) on a stretch of the East Coast Main Line between Northallerton and Thirsk, North Yorkshire. The record was broken in 1987 by the InterCity 125, when a speed of 148mph (238km/h) was reached over a measured mile between York and Northallerton.

World's longest railway platform bench

Scarborough railway station

Scarborough station in North Yorkshire is home to what is said to be the world's longest railway bench. To be found on Platform 1, the wooden painted seat runs for 152 yards (139m). One day in 2016, between 400 and 500 primary school children sat on the bench for a reading project. There are unconfirmed reports that the record for longest railway bench has recently been broken.

Below: Scarborough railway station is home to what is said to be the longest railway platform bench in the world

Most countries visited in twenty-four hours by scheduled transport

A modern-day Phileas Fogg, Adam Leyton of Horsforth, West Yorkshire, passed through twelve countries during a whistle-stop tour of Europe using only planes, trains and buses. He started in Germany and journeyed through Luxembourg, France, Belgium, the Netherlands, Denmark, Sweden, Poland, the Czech Republic, Slovakia, Hungary and Austria. The journey in May 2016 beat the previous record of eleven countries and was validated in 2017 by Guinness World Records.

Longest time in bed

The rather tragic character of William Sharp, of Laycock, near Keighley, West Yorkshire, was jilted at the altar and chose to spend the rest of his life in bed. His lie-in lasted for forty-nine years until his death in 1856. During that time he was in a bedroom measuring approximately 9ft^2, with virtually no furniture. The window was never opened and Sharp never spoke to a soul, ignoring even the person who brought him his meals. It is said he remained remarkably healthy despite his horizontal lifestyle.

Longest time out of bed

Christopher Pivett, a carver and gilder in York, spent the last thirty-eight years of his life out of bed. After his house had burnt down in 1746 he resolved to never again lie on a bed. He slept, instead, on the floor, or upon a chair. It seemed to do him no harm for he died aged ninety-three years.

Britain's largest clothing manufacturer

In the 1920s, Joseph Hepworth & Son of Leeds was the largest clothing manufacturer in the United Kingdom. The company's name was changed to Next in the 1980s.

Longest time spent underground

Geoff Workman entered the record books in 1963 when he spent 105 days living 100ft (30.5m) underground. His feat of endurance, at the Stump Cross Caverns, North Yorkshire, smashed the previous world record. At the time it was thought to be beyond human endurance to live underground for so long. The record has since been broken.

Britain's highest lake

At 1,237ft (377m) above sea level, Malham Tarn, North Yorkshire, is said to be the highest marl lake in the United Kingdom.

Britain's oldest working cable tramway

Dating back to 1895, the Shipley Glen Cable Tramway is the oldest working cable tramway in Britain (cliff lifts excepted). The line was constructed to serve the local beauty spot of Shipley Glen, near Saltaire, West Yorkshire.

England's first athlete

Foster Powell, born in Horsforth, West Yorkshire, is regarded as "the first English athlete of whom we have any record". Known as the "great pedestrian", he walked great distances in the mid-1700s, making a living from wagers.

World's first Fairtrade crisps

Made from plantain rather than potatoes, the world's first Fairtrade-certified crisps were introduced by Bradford-based Premcrest in 2013. The plantain used originated in the Amazonian region of Equador.

Keighley was half of the first twinning

World's first recorded town twinning agreement

Keighley holds the honour of being one half of the first recorded town twinning agreement in the world. The West Yorkshire town first twinned with Poix-du-Nord, France, in 1920. The practice was originally described not as town twinning but as an adoption of the French town. An earlier twinning arrangement between Keighley and Suresnes and Puteaux, also in France, began in 1905.

World's first Fairtrade Village

The Brontë village of Haworth, West Yorkshire, became the first to be awarded Fairtrade status by the Fairtrade Foundation on 22 November 2002.

World's first virtual newsreader

Ananova

In April 2000, the Press Association launched Ananova, the world's first virtual newscaster. Broadcasting to the world from Leeds, Ananova was an internet-based 3D rendered model who read the news with a mid-Atlantic accent. She was given a distinctive look and personality based on celebrities Victoria Beckham, Kylie Minogue, and Carol Vorderman. Ananova's character was discontinued in 2004 and the name Ananova disappeared in 2010.

Ananova, the world's first virtual newsreader

World's first robot lawyer

Harrogate solicitor Chrissie Lightfoot created the world's first robot lawyer in 2017. Called LISA, the artificial intelligence-based system could draft legally binding documents, bypassing the need for a human lawyer.

World's longest domestic cat

In October 2015, Ludo, a Maine Coon breed cat from Wakefield measured a whopping 3ft 10.59in (118.33cm) long, taking the world record. A vet measured the moggy during filming of ITV documentary *The Story of Cats*. The super-sized pet is owned by Kelsey Gill.

World's fastest coin-operated ride

A coin-operated Postman Pat delivery van, driven by Ben Rushworth of Leeds, took PAT 1 a quarter of a mile in 12.071 seconds at York Raceway in September 2011.

Reaching speeds of more than 100mph (161km/h), the modified little red van recorded a better time than super cars such as the Porsche 911.

World's fastest tortoise

Charlie the tortoise held the world speed record for a remarkable thirty-eight years. He set the record by travelling 18ft (5.4m) in 43.7 seconds at the National Tortoise Championships at Tickhill, South Yorkshire, in 1977. The record held until 2015.

World's first gritter museum

In 2012 the world's first museum dedicated to gritters opened its doors in Ripon. Vintage snowploughs and spreaders were put on show. Highlights included a beautifully restored Army 1972 Bedford gritter with red, white and blue Jubilee livery.

Britain's highest rainfall

According to the Met Office, two separate West Yorkshire locations may hold the record for the highest 120-minute total rainfall in the UK. On 19th May 1989, 7.6in (193mm) of rain was recorded at Walshaw Dean Lodge. However, as the Met Office has "reservations" about the figure, the next highest accepted value was 6.1in (155mm) measured on 11th June 1956 at Hewenden Reservoir.

Britain's warmest September day

On 2nd September, 1906, at Hesley Hall, Bawtry, South Yorkshire, a temperature of 35.6°C (96.1°F) was registered – a UK record for a September temperature.

World's longest-established cave rescue team

The world's longest-established cave rescue team was formed in the Yorkshire Dales in 1935. The Clapham-based Cave Rescue Organisation has since come to the aid of several thousand people.

World's first saucy seaside postcard

The original saucy seaside postcards were created by Bamforth & Co of Holmfirth, West Yorkshire. At their peak in the 1930s, sixteen million were sold each year.

Britain's oldest dinner lady

Described by the national press as Britain's oldest dinner lady, Jean Artt turned eighty in 2015 and was still serving up school dinners at the Unity City Academy, Middlesbrough, North Yorkshire. She had spent forty-eight years as a dinner nanny, serving more than 9,000 children, and said she had no plans to retire.

The world's first saucy postcards were produced in Holmfirth

Britain's least successful Parliamentary candidate

World's fastest knitter

In 1980 Gwen Matthewman, of Streethouse, near Wakefield, broke the official world record for knitting. She could knit at a speed of 111 stitches per minute. She was also the world's most prolific hand knitter after creating 915 garments from 11,000oz (312kg) of wool in a year.

R Lees stood for parliament at a by-election held in Ripon, North Yorkshire, in 1860. He is believed to be the only candidate in British history to receive zero votes.

England's largest cow

The Craven Heifer (1807–1812) remains the largest cow ever shown in England. The heifer was bred by the Reverend William Carr in 1807, on the Duke of Devonshire's estate at Bolton Abbey, North Yorkshire. She weighed 312 stone (two tonnes), and measured 11ft 4in (3.45m) in length and over 7ft (2.13m) in height.

Europe's oldest West Indian carnival

The Leeds Carnival, held in the Chapeltown and Harehills areas of Leeds, has been held since 1967, making it the longest-running West Indian carnival in Europe.

England's largest hill figure

The Kilburn White Horse, in the North York Moors, is said to be the largest and most northerly hill figure in England. Measuring 318ft (97m) long by 220ft (67m) high, it covers about 1.6 acres (6,475m²). On a clear day it can be seen twenty-eight miles (45km) away, in North Leeds.

The white horse was created in November 1857 by a group of pupils and other volunteers led by local schoolmaster John Hodgson.

World's first cat's eye

The reflective roadstuds known as cat's eyes, now found in their millions down the centre of the world's roads, were invented in 1933 by Percy Shaw, of Boothtown, Halifax, West Yorkshire. He patented his invention in 1934 and a year later founded Reflecting Roadstuds Limited in Halifax to manufacture Catseyes, the company's trademark. In 2006 the cat's eye was included alongside Concorde, the K2 telephone box and the World Wide Web as one of Britain's top ten design icons.

Britain's first mobile phone call

The first official UK mobile phone call was made by Leeds-born comedian Ernie Wise on New Year's Day 1985.

World's only remaining gas-lit cinema

The Hyde Park Picture House, Leeds, is thought to be the last cinema in the world still to be lit by gas.

World's first bike libraries

A scheme started by Yorkshire Bank in 2014 sees people donate unwanted bikes, which are refurbished and offered for hire free of charge. The aim of the project is that every child in the county should be able to access a bicycle.

World's largest parade of scooters

The Yorkshire Scooter Alliance drove a parade of 864 scooters across the Humber Bridge, in the East Riding, on 14th August 2010. A further four took part but they could not be included as they drove behind a support vehicle.

World's fastest monowheel motorcycle

The top speed achieved on a monowheel motorcycle was recorded at Elvington Airfield, North Yorkshire, in September 2015. The speed of 61.18mph (98.46km/h) was reached by Kevin Scott riding WarHorse.

Mike Newman drove at over 200mph while blindfolded

Greatest distance covered on a treadmill

Fastest speed for a car driven blindfolded

On August 2014, Mike Newman drove a car at just over 200mph (322.69km/h) while blindfolded. His record-breaking drive took place at Elvington Airfield, North Yorkshire.

Sharon Gayter ran 517.63 miles (833.05km) on a treadmill in one week at Teesside University, Middlesbrough, North Yorkshire, between 14th and 21st December 2011.

World's first triple transplant patient

The first person to receive a heart-lung-liver transplant was Davina Thompson, of Rawmarsh, near Rotherham, South Yorkshire. In December 1986, over a period of seven hours, she underwent the groundbreaking surgery, performed by a team of fifteen, at Papworth Hospital, Cambridge. She died, aged forty-seven, in August 1998.

Britain's first hand transplant

Mark Cahill

On Boxing Day 2012, grandfather Mark Cahill of Halifax, West Yorkshire, became the first UK person to receive a hand transplant. The pioneering surgery was conducted by plastic surgeon Simon Kay at Leeds General Infirmary and took eight hours. Fifty-one-year-old Mark said afterwards: "The operation has changed my life. Before the op, I couldn't tie my own shoes, do up the buttons on my shirt, cut up my own dinner or play with my grandson's toys with him – hopefully I'll be able to do all these things now." Two years later, Mark used his new limb to save his wife's life after she suffered a heart attack. He said it was only because of his hand transplant that he was able to perform chest compressions on Sylvia, fifty-one. He said: "I knew getting my hand would be life-changing but I never thought it would be life-saving as well."

World's oldest person to have a total hip replacement

John Lawrence Randall of Pontefract, West Yorkshire, had his left hip replaced at the grand age of 102. He underwent the two-hour operation so he could continue his hobby of gardening. As it was the second time he had received a new left hip, the operation was far more complex. His granddaughter Gillian Coates said he had "true Yorkshire determination". The replacement was carried out at Pinderfields Hospital in Wakefield on 15 November 2011. There are reports the record has since been broken.

Largest game of If You're Happy and You Know It

In Lister Park, Manningham, Bradford, on 7th July 2011, a whopping 1,128 schoolchildren joined in with a mass rendition of the action-based children's rhyme.

Most bedding plants planted in one hour by an individual

Steven Thorpe planted a remarkable 2,021 bedding plants in just one hour at Haworth Central Park, Haworth, West Yorkshire, on 21st October 2006.

Record for 24-hour tandem indoor rowing

In July 2010, Julian Norton, best known as television's The Yorkshire Vet, and Roger Brown set a new indoor rowing record at Thirsk Leisure Centre, North Yorkshire, reaching 226.45 miles (364.44km), rowing non-stop in tandem over a twenty-four hour period.

First woman to fly solo to Australia

Amy Johnson

In 1930, Hull-born Amy Johnson became the first woman to fly solo from Britain to Australia. It was a feat that won her widespread fame and adulation.

She would go on to break numerous other aviation records before her early death, aged just thirty-seven, after bailing out of a stricken aeroplane in 1941.

Inset and below:
Amy Johnson

World's first manned flight

George Cayley

Although the powered flight made by the Wright brothers fifty years later is far better known, the first manned flight, in what was essentially an aeroplane, took place in Yorkshire in 1853 at Brompton Dale, near Scarborough, North Yorkshire.

Right: a diagram of Cayley's glider design

Pioneering aviator George Cayley invented a glider capable of carrying a man

Pioneering aviator George Cayley, who had been working on putting man into the air since 1804, invented a glider capable of carrying a man and later theorised how it could be powered using a hot-air motor. The first passenger on one of his gliders was an unidentified boy of about ten years old who flew

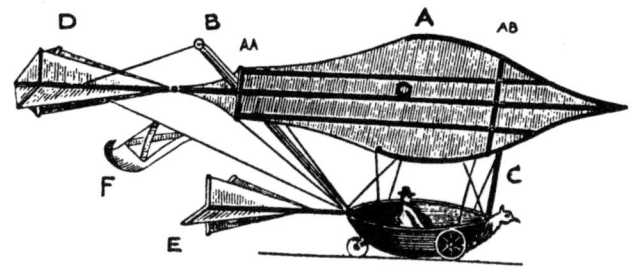

Fⁱ𝗴. 1

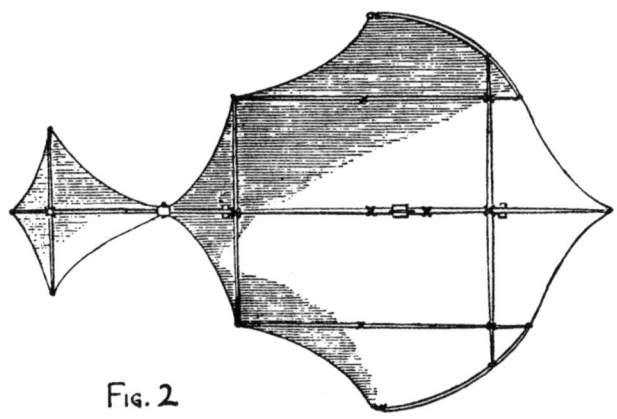

Fⁱ𝗴. 2

successfully for several feet some time before 1849. Sadly the
name of the first adult to fly in a heavier-than-air machine is
also not known for certain. It was not Cayley, then seventy-nine
years old – and reports varyingly credit his groom/coachman
John Appleby or his grandson. Cayley called his glider The
Governable Parachute. A life-size replica of the 1853 glider was
made at Brough, near Hull, to celebrate the 150th anniversary
of the first manned flight. Sir Richard Branson piloted the
machine at Brompton Dale in July 2003.

Britain's first astronaut

Dr Helen Sharman, born in Grenoside, Sheffield, became the first British astronaut and the first woman to visit the Mir space station in 1991. She responded to a radio ad asking for applicants to be the first British astronaut and was selected for the mission live on ITV on 25th November 1989, ahead of almost 13,000 other applicants.

World's most tattooed female senior citizen

Born in Mytholmroyd, West Yorkshire, Isobel Varley got her first tattoo aged forty-seven and loved it so much she had to have more. She went on to have 200 pieces completed in ten years. By the time of her death in 2015, aged seventy-seven, she had ninety-three per cent of her body inked. Her favourite tattoos were a family of tigers on her stomach. "Originally, I was only ever going to have one – a small bird – but I fell in love with it, and developed an addiction," she told Guinness World Records after being handed her title. "The only areas not completely tattooed are my face, soles of my feet, my ears and some area on my hands."

England's largest underground chamber

Measuring 322ft (98m) deep, the pothole Gaping Gill in Ingleborough, North Yorkshire, is England's largest underground chamber naturally open to the surface. It also holds the record for the highest unbroken waterfall in England (see p54).

Britain's largest chimney

The reinforced concrete chimney at Drax Power Station, North Yorkshire, stands 850ft (259m) high, with a diameter of 30ft (9.1m), and weighs 44,000 tonnes. When first built, it was the largest industrial chimney in the world, and is still the tallest in the UK.

World's largest factory

In its day, Armley Mills, in Armley, west Leeds, was the world's largest woollen mill and probably also the world's largest factory. Now home to the Leeds Industrial Museum, the current structures were built in 1805 by Benjamin Gott and closed as a commercial mill in 1969.

Oldest British flying aeroplane

The Blackburn Type D was constructed by Robert Blackburn at Leeds in 1912. The single-engine mid-wing monoplane remains part of the Shuttleworth Collection and is the oldest British flyable aeroplane.

World's largest industrial building

When first built in 1853, Salts Mill, at Saltaire, West Yorkshire, was said to be the largest industrial building in the world by total floor area.

Britain's most powerful power station

Drax coal-fired power station in North Yorkshire has a generating capacity of 3,960 megawatts, the highest of any power station in the United Kingdom.

World's first film

On October 1888, French cinematographer Louis Le Prince captured the first ever moving pictures, using a camera that he went on to patent. He filmed members of his family walking around a garden in the Leeds suburb of Roundhay. The films of Le Prince predate those of the better-known Thomas Edison and the Lumière brothers.

Having perfected his projection machine, the film-maker planned to demonstrate his moving pictures to the American public in New York City in 1890. But just weeks before the trip, he mysteriously disappeared. Because his body was never recovered, his family had to wait seven years before he was declared legally dead. In the interim, Edison and the Lumières completed their work, claiming the resultant fame and fortune. Until recently, Le Prince's achievements have been relatively forgotten, though a documentary, *The First Film*, has helped restore his name to the public consciousness.

World's first UNESCO City of Film

The metropolitan district of Bradford has been the backdrop for famous films such as *The Railway Children* and *The King's Speech*. It is also home to the National Science and Media Museum, which houses three cinemas, including the UK's first IMAX high-resolution film theatre. Because of this rich film heritage, Bradford was the first location to receive the title of UNESCO City of Film in June 2009, followed a year later by Sydney, Australia.

World's first film edit

Bamforth & Co, of Holmfirth, West Yorkshire, is believed to have invented film editing with its 1899 film *The Kiss in the Tunnel*.

Britain's oldest working theatre

The Georgian Theatre Royal, Richmond

The Georgian Theatre Royal, in Richmond, North Yorkshire, is the country's oldest working theatre in its original form. It is also Britain's most complete Georgian playhouse. Built in 1788 by actor-manager Samuel Butler, it was in regular use until 1830. In 1848 it became an auction room and wine vaults were constructed in the pit at about the same time. In 1963 the Grade I Listed building was reopened following a public appeal and restoration. A second extensive restoration took place in 2002.

The Georgian Theatre Royal is Britain's most complete Georgian playhouse

The theatre has a capacity of 214, with the audience arranged in rectangular form with sunken pit, boxes on three sides and a small gallery above. The theatre is also holder of another UK record. It is the owner of Britain's oldest set of scenery, "The Woodland Scene", which was painted between 1818 and 1836. Actor Peter Davison said of the theatre: "It should be listed as one of the wonders of the world, in my book."

World's first male supermodel

John Pearson

Described as the world's first male supermodel by the *Sunday Times*, *Daily Telegraph*, *Vogue* magazine and the *New York Post*, John Pearson was first spotted by a photographer at eighteen, while working at a denim shop in his native Sheffield.

After posing for the cover of Self *magazine with Uma Thurman, his career blossomed*

By 1986, aged twenty-one, Pearson left Yorkshire for New York City. After posing for the cover of *Self* magazine with Uma Thurman, his career blossomed, and in 1990 he was cast in George Michael's *Freedom! '90* music video, co-starring Cindy Crawford, Naomi Campbell, Linda Evangelista, Christy Turlington and Tatjana Patitz. He is the only male model to appear in *American GQ* editorials across three decades.

Europe's largest open-air theatre

Scarborough Open Air Theatre in North Yorkshire, which has a capacity of 6,500, is the largest in Europe.

World's biggest offshore windfarm

The world's biggest offshore windfarm is currently being constructed off the Yorkshire coast near Hornsea. On completion in the 2020s, the multi-billion-pound project will cover an area five times the size of Hull, with 300 turbines each taller than the Gherkin in London.

World's biggest business card

Measuring 728 times the area of a normal business card, printing company Instantprint in Rotherham, South Yorkshire, created the world's largest business card in 2015, breaking the official world record. The card measured 7.5ft (2.3m) by 5ft (1.5m). Business co-owner James Kinsella, whose name was on the card, said: "I think it's a childhood dream, for most people, to achieve a world record."

World's oldest Classic horse race

First run in 1776, the annual St Ledger Stakes takes place at Doncaster, South Yorkshire, in September, over one mile, six furlongs and 132 yards (2.94km). It is the oldest and longest of Britain's five Classics.

It was devised by Anthony St Leger, an Army officer and MP who organised the inaugural two-mile running.

Britain's first horse race for women

Ripon, North Yorkshire, is believed to have staged Britain's first horse race for female riders in 1723.

England's oldest annual horse race

The Kiplingcotes Derby

The Kiplingcotes Derby was reputedly first raced in 1519 and has taken place on the third Thursday in March every year since. It takes place across arduous farm tracks and fields at Kiplingcotes, near Market Weighton, in the East Riding.

The rules state that if the race is not run one year then it must never be run again

The original rules, which are still strictly adhered to, state that if the race is not run one year then it must never be run again. In order to ensure its future, during the snowstorms of 1947, one brave local farmer led a horse around the course. The same happened in 2001 when the spread of foot-and-mouth disease prevented the movement of animals.

Europe's longest continuous racecourse

Pontefract Racecourse, West Yorkshire, is the longest continuous circuit in Europe at two miles and 125 yards (3.3km) long.

World's largest portion of fish and chips

The Wensleydale Heifer, West Witton

On July 2011, the Wensleydale Heifer, in the Dales village of West Witton, North Yorkshire, broke the world record for a serving of fish and chips. The pub battered the previous record-holder (which, to rub salt in the wounds of all Tykes, was a restaurant in America) with a mountain of deep-fried grub. A 40lb (18.1kg) fillet of prime halibut was fried in more than four gallons (18.1 litres) of Black Sheep beer batter, alongside 60lb (27.2kg) of hand-cut chips and a vat of mushy peas.

World's largest fish and chip shop

Opening in January 2017, Papas Fish & Chips in Scarborough, North Yorkshire, claims to be the world's biggest fish and chip restaurant, with seating for 450 customers. Harry Ramsden's, of Guiseley, West Yorkshire, once held the world record, seating 250 people and serving nearly a million customers a year. The resultant annual shopping list included 264,000lb (119.75 tonnes) of haddock, 660,000lb (299 tonnes) of potatoes and 20,000 bottles of sauce.

Most portions of fish and chips sold in a single day

Harry Ramsden's, at Guiseley, West Yorkshire, twice broke the world record for selling the most portions of fish and chips in a single day. On 7th July, 1952, to mark the restaurant's twenty-first birthday, fish and chips were sold at 1912 prices. As a result, 10,000 portions were served up. In 1988, when prices were again dropped to celebrate the restaurant's diamond jubilee, the record was broken again, with 11,964 portions served up to hungry patrons.

World's largest ball of cling film

In November 2013, a team at Hessle Road Network Young People's Centre, in Hull, made a giant ball of cling film, weighing 470lb (213.2kg).

Longest ongoing tradition in the world

The Ripon Wakeman

Above: the Ripon Wakeman

Every evening at 9pm the Wakeman of Ripon, North Yorkshire, sounds a horn to set the watch for the city. The ancient ceremony dates back to the year 886 when Alfred the Great visited Ripon and granted the community a Royal Charter, in the form of a ceremonial horn. From that day the horn was blown by the man appointed Wakeman, whose job it was to check the city was safe during the evening.

The ancient ceremony dates back to 886

Generation after generation has kept the tradition alive. It is, according to the website of George Pickles – the Ripon City Hornblower from 2003 to 2015 – "the longest ongoing tradition in the world". It is certainly a contender.

World's oldest football club

Sheffield FC

Officially established in 1857, Sheffield FC was the world's first association football club. Founders Nathaniel Creswick and William Prest also wrote the first set of football rules, the Sheffield rules, which became the basis of the modern game of football. The first derby was played in 1860 following the founding of another Sheffield team, Hallam FC.

When, in 1885, professional football arrived in England, Sheffield FC chose not to pay its players, founding instead the first official amateur football competition, the FA Amateur Cup. The club has stuck by its principles and has always been operated on a non-professional basis.

Sheffield FC, 1890

World's oldest recorded sporting event

Organisers of the Antient Silver Arrow claim the archery contest, held annually in Scorton, North Yorkshire, is the world's longest established and oldest recorded sporting event. Dating back to 1673, the competition is open to any Gentleman Archer aged over twenty-one shooting in the long bow or any other bar bow. Only wars have stopped the event taking place each year. Several other sporting events claim to have been running for longer than the Antient Scorton Silver Arrow but its records are said to go back the furthest.

World's oldest football stadium

Opened in 1855, Bramall Lane, home of Sheffield United, is the oldest major stadium in the world still to be hosting professional association football matches.

World's first floodlit football match

Bramall Lane, Sheffield, hosted the first ever floodlit football match in 1878.

Most cricket overs delivered

Members of Rodley Cricket Club, in Leeds, delivered 734 cricket overs in eight hours at the club's annual open weekend in August 2016. Thirty-three bowlers took part, with fifty-three people performing batting duties.

First County Championship match

The first ever official cricket County Championship match began on 12 May 1890. The winners, Yorkshire, beat Gloucestershire by eight wickets at Bristol.

Most wickets taken in first-class cricket

Wilfred Rhodes, of Kirkheaton, West Yorkshire, took 4,204 first-class wickets in 1,100 matches, playing for Yorkshire CCC and England between 1898 and 1930.

Most county titles

Yorkshire has won by far the most county titles, with thirty-two outright titles and one shared at the time of writing.

Fewest runs conceded while taking all ten wickets in a single innings

In July 1932, Hedley Verity, the Yorkshire CCC bowler who was a native of Headingley, Leeds, set a first-class record that remains unbroken. In a match against Nottinghamshire he conceded just ten runs in the process of taking all ten wickets in an innings.

World's first Rugby League teams

Rugby League was created at a meeting at the George Hotel, Huddersfield, West Yorkshire, on 29th August 1895, leading to the establishment of the first teams.

Biggest attendance for a Rugby League match

The record attendance for a rugby league game was at the 1954 Rugby League Cup Final Replay. The crunch match between Halifax and Warrington was held at the Odsal Stadium, Bradford. Officially the crowd was recorded at 102,575 but estimates say the actual figure could have been as high as 120,000. As the match began there were still thousands of latecomers streaming into the stadium – the roads for miles around had been gridlocked for hours.

Longest frame in professional snooker history

In April 2017, at the Ponds Forge International Sports Centre in Sheffield, the deciding frame between Fergal O'Brien and David Gilbert lasted two hours, three minutes and forty-one seconds. That's forty-four seconds longer than the record for a men's marathon. O'Brien said: "Obviously in an ideal world you win a bit quicker than that."

Yorkshire has won thirty-two outright county titles

Longest rugby try in history

Players and supporters of Wensleydale RUFC, North Yorkshire, completed the longest try when they ran the ball from Wensleydale to Twickenham, the home of English rugby. The six-day, 245-mile (394.3km) relay was completed by nine participants, led by Second XV captain Dave Piper, in November 2016.

Britain's first Tour de France hero

Brian Robinson, of Mirfield, West Yorkshire, was the first Briton to win a stage of the Tour de France in 1958. He repeated the feat in 1959.

Greatest British female cyclist of all time

Beryl Burton of Halton, Leeds, won more than nine domestic championships and seven world titles, and set numerous national records. She set a women's record for the twelve-hour time-trial which exceeded the men's record for two years. She is widely regarded as the greatest British female cyclist of all time.

Britain's oldest sauropod dinosaur

A fossil bone recently found near Whitby, North Yorkshire, provides the earliest skeletal record of a sauropod dinosaur in Britain. The backbone of the dinosaur, nicknamed "Alan" after the finder, Alan Gurr, was from a group of reptile-footed dinosaurs that includes the largest land animals to have ever roamed the Earth. They had long necks and tails, small heads, a large body and would have walked on all fours. Professor Phil Manning and his Manchester University team said: "Many scientists have worked on the amazing dinosaur tracks from the Middle Jurassic rocks of Yorkshire. It was a splendid surprise to come face-to-face with a fossil vertebra from the Jurassic rocks of Yorkshire that was clearly from a sauropod dinosaur."

Dr Victoria Egerton added that the Jurassic Park that is now Yorkshire "clearly has much more to offer science in our understanding of the distribution and evolution of dinosaurs."

World's first seaside resort

Scarborough

People have been flocking to enjoy the delights of sunny Scarborough, North Yorkshire, for almost 400 years and it is probably the world's oldest seaside resort. It is almost certainly the first in Britain. Tourists were first drawn to the town for the health-giving properties of a stream of acidic spa water that flowed down one of the cliffs. Tourists began visiting the town for bathing excursions shortly before 1720 and the first rolling bathing machines – mobile changing rooms – were introduced as early as 1736. The town really boomed following the arrival of the railway in 1845.

Largest purpose-built hotel in Europe

The Grand Hotel, Scarborough, with its 413 rooms over twelve floors, was the largest purpose-built hotel in Europe when it first opened in 1867.

World's oldest visitor attraction

Mother Shipton's Cave

Open since 1630, England's oldest entrance-charging tourist attraction is Mother Shipton's Cave, at Knaresborough, North Yorkshire. The cave has a long association with the famed prophetess Mother Shipton, born Ursula Southeil, who reputedly predicted the Great Fire of London. She was said to have been born in the cave, and returned there later in life. Nearby is a petrifying well, which has also helped draw the tourists down the centuries.

Mother Shipton's Cave

Most sandcastles built in an hour

Scarborough

An estimated 400 people constructed 683 sandcastles on the beach at South Bay, Scarborough, North Yorkshire, in August 2012. The previous record crumbled as the Scarborough event, organised by Yorkshire Water, beat it by more than 100 castles. Each of the sandcastles had to be 2ft (61cm) tall, with a 2ft (61cm)-wide base, and include four intact turrets.

Below: the record attempt for most sandcastles in an hour on the beach at Scarborough

World's first nature reserve

Walton Hall, near Wakefield

The world's first modern nature reserve was created in 1821 by Yorkshire-born explorer and naturalist Charles Waterton. He spent £9,000 on the construction of a three-mile (4.83km)-long, 9ft (2.74m)-tall wall around his estate at Walton Hall, near Wakefield. He also planted trees, and hollowed out trunks to house owls. He tried to introduce little owls from Italy and created birdhouses to attract species such as starlings, jackdaws and sand martins. According to David Attenborough, he was "one of the first people anywhere to recognise not only that the natural world was of great importance but that it needed protection as humanity made more and more demands on it".

Charles Waterton

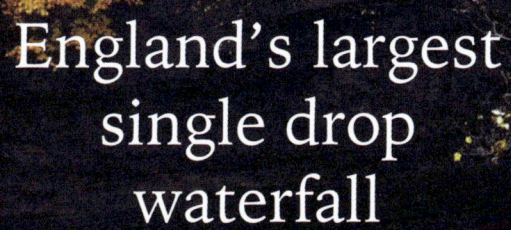

England's largest single drop waterfall

Hardraw Force

Tumbling approximately 100ft (30m), Hardraw Force, North Yorkshire, is said to be England's highest unbroken waterfall. Privately owned and recently put up for sale, access to this wonder of nature is through the bar of the Green Dragon Inn in Hardraw. An entrance fee is payable in the pub.

The waterfall was visited by both JMW Turner and William Wordsworth and more recently it appeared in the film *Robin Hood: Prince of Thieves* in a scene where Maid Marian (Mary Elizabeth Mastrantonio) catches Robin Hood (Kevin Costner) bathing underneath the fall.

England's highest cascading waterfall above ground

The broken cascade of falls called Cautley Spout tumbles a total of 650ft (198m). It is located near Sedbergh in the West Riding.

Largest brick structure in Europe

When it was built in 1867, the Grand Hotel, in Scarborough, North Yorkshire, was the largest brick structure in Europe.

England's highest waterfall (above and below ground)

The waterfall inside Gaping Gill, a natural cave on the southern slopes of Ingleborough, in the Yorkshire Dales (North Yorkshire), is the highest unbroken waterfall in the country, measuring approximately 322ft (98m). The water comes from the Fell Beck, which flows into the pothole.

England's largest village

A number of communities make this claim, based on either acreage or population. In the nineteenth century, Horsforth was said to be the most populous in England. These days, Ecclesfield, South Yorkshire, with 32,073 residents, is said to be the country's most populous parish. On the basis of geographical size, Bradfield, South Yorkshire, Hunmanby, North Yorkshire, Rawmarsh, South Yorkshire, and Cottingham, East Riding of Yorkshire, each has claims on the title of England's largest village.

Britain's most picturesque street

Although beauty is in the eye of the beholder, making it rather hard to quantify, York's Shambles has been voted Britain's most picturesque on at least two separate occasions. The historic city thoroughfare came top in polls in 2010 and 2017. The street is also thought to be the best-preserved medieval street in Europe.

World's most performed living playwright

Alan Ayckbourn, based in Scarborough, North Yorkshire, has written and produced more than seventy full-length plays and is said to be the world's most performed living playwright.

England's longest medieval town walls

York's City Walls are 2.1 miles (3.4km) long. The beautifully preserved walls are visited by an estimated 2.5 million people each year and a walk of the entire circuit takes approximately two hours. It has been estimated that the walls weigh approximately 100,000 metric tonnes.

World's longest railway tunnel

When completed in 1841, the Summit Tunnel, near Todmorden, West Yorkshire, was the longest railway tunnel in the world. Mined by hand, it is just over 1.6 miles (2.6km) long.

Britain's steepest flight of canal locks

The Bingley Five-Rise Locks on the Leeds and Liverpool Canal at Bingley, West Yorkshire, are the steepest in the UK, with a gradient of about 1:5. The gates at the bottom of the rise are said to be the tallest in Britain.

World's longest remaining transporter bridge

The Tees Transporter Bridge across the River Tees in Middlesbrough, North Yorkshire, has an overall length of 851ft (259m), with a span between the centres of the towers of 590ft (180m), making it the world's longest remaining transporter bridge.

Bingley Five-Rise Locks is the steepest in the UK

Britain's tallest permanent maypole

The Otley maypole, in the West Yorkshire town's Manchester Square, measures 75ft (22.8m) in height. A further 12ft (3.6m) is below ground. It was controversially taken down in 2014 due to safety fears, but replaced nine months later.

Europe's longest roller coaster

Costing £5.2 million to build, the Ultimate roller coaster at Lightwater Valley theme park near Ripon, North Yorkshire, was the longest in the world when it opened in 1991. It held the record until 2000, when a Japanese 'coaster took the title. Spanning 1.4 miles (2.2km), it remains the longest in Europe.

Britain's longest, deepest and highest canal tunnel

The Standedge Tunnel beneath the Pennines, on the Huddersfield Narrow Canal, West Yorkshire, is the longest and highest in the UK. It is 5,500 yards (5,000m) long, 636ft (194m) underground at its deepest point, and 643ft (196m) above sea level.

Britain's furthest inland port

The docks at Goole, in the West Riding, make up Britain's furthest inland port, though Selby also has a claim on the title.

England's highest motorway

At 1,221ft (372m) above sea level, the M62 at Windy Hill near Saddleworth Moor, in the West Riding, is the highest point of any motorway in England.

World's largest hockey lesson

On 21st March 2015, at Cundall Manor School, Cundall, North Yorkshire, 498 students and eleven coaches took part in the world's largest field hockey lesson.

Britain's longest single-span suspension bridge

The Humber Bridge

Work began on the Humber Bridge, across the Humber Estuary, in 1973. Traffic first crossed the bridge in July 1981 after the Queen performed the formal opening ceremony.

A remarkable feat of engineering, it was the longest of its type in the world, holding on to the record until 1998. It is now the world's eighth-longest single-span suspension bridge, but remains the longest in Britain. Measuring 7,280ft (2,220m) in length, as of 2006, the bridge carried an average of 120,000 vehicles per week. Including interest, the Humber Bridge cost £151,000,000 to build. It is said to still be the world's longest single-span suspension bridge that can be crossed by foot.

Discovery of oxygen

Clergyman Joseph Priestley, of Birstall, West Yorkshire, discovered oxygen. He isolated it in its gaseous state and published the first report describing its properties in 1775, before other scientists with a claim to the discovery. Priestley noted that candles burned brighter in what he called "dephlogisticated air" and that a mouse was more active and lived longer while breathing it. Priestley also investigated electricity and invented soda water.

First English poet

The earliest English poet whose name is known is the Anglo Saxon Cædmon, who cared for animals at Whitby Abbey, North Yorkshire.

His "song of creation" was the first English poem.

Discovery of stainless steel

Harry Brearley invented what he called "rustless steel" in August 1913, transforming the cutlery industry of his home city, Sheffield.

First European to reach eastern coastline of Australia

Captain James Cook of Marton, North Yorkshire, now a suburb of Middlesbrough, achieved many firsts but he is best known for being the first European to make contact with the eastern coastline of Australia. Among his other achievements was the first recorded circumnavigation of New Zealand.

England's smallest window

The George Hotel, Hull

Blink and you'd miss it. A small plaque beside what appears to be a crack in the wall declares it to be, in actual fact, "England's smallest window". The plaque is installed on the wall of The George Hotel in the curiously named Land of Green Ginger, a narrow street in the old town area of Hull.

The plaque explains: "The George Hotel is one of Hull's oldest surviving public houses and can be dated back to 1685. It is also home to England's smallest window which is rumoured to have been used in the days when The George was a coaching inn. A porter was seated in the window to watch for the coaches so as to give immediate attention on arrival."

England's smallest house

A tiny, one-room house with no toilet is said to be England's smallest house. The residence on Denholme Road, Oxenhope, West Yorkshire, dates back to 1871. Measuring 13ft 6in (4.1m) by 10ft 6in (3.2m), original features include a gas light, stone flag floor and ceramic floor.

Named Little Dorrit, the detached house boasts stunning views. Previous uses have included a communal wash house, pie shop and toll house. It was built by a retired dragoon guard. In 2005 the house sold for £15,000.

Another building with a claim on the title is a tiny half-timbered house adjoining All Saints Church in North Street, York.

England's smallest stately home

The diminutive Grade II listed Ebberston Hall, North Yorkshire, is said to be England's smallest stately home. It was built in 1718.

Britain's largest private house

Wentworth Woodhouse, the Grade I listed country house near Rotherham, South Yorkshire, is the largest in the UK. It is home to more than 300 rooms, with 250,000ft^2 (23,000m^2) of floorspace. It covers an area of more than 2.5 acres (1ha).

Europe's longest country house façade

With an east front of 606ft (185m), Wentworth Woodhouse, South Yorkshire, has Europe's longest country house façade.

England's oldest inhabited village

Rudston, East Riding of Yorkshire

There are a number of challengers to the title, but Rudston, nestling on the edge of the Yorkshire Wolds, is often described as England's oldest inhabited village. In the village churchyard stands the Rudston Monolith, or rood-stone, from which the village probably takes it name. The main street passing through the village is an ancient route that may have been in use since Neolithic times.

Britain's tallest standing stone

Rudston Monolith

The Rudston Monolith, in the village of Rudston, stands at 25ft (7.6m), making it the tallest megalith, or standing stone, in the United Kingdom. The top appears to have broken off and if pointed, the monolith would have originally reached to about 28ft (8.5m). The monument dates to the Late Neolithic or Early Bronze Age period and there are unsubstantiated claims that a fossilised dinosaur footprint is on one side of the stone.

The real size of the giant stone may be even greater still. From experiments made early in the eighteenth century, archaeologist Sir William Strickland was said to have found: "the dimensions of the monolith within ground as large as those without".

World's largest room

At the time it was first constructed, it was said that Temple Works – a flax mill in Holbeck, Leeds – was the biggest single room in the world.

World's longest terraced street

The village of Altofts, West Yorkshire, was home to the longest unbroken row of three-storey terraced houses in Europe, Silkstone Row, until 1978 when it was demolished.

Britain's oldest house

The oldest house in the UK was unearthed by archeologists in 2010. Carbon dating has revealed that the building at Star Carr near Scarborough, North Yorkshire, stood in 8,500BC, when Britain was still connected to continental Europe. Measuring 11.5ft (3.5m) wide, the house was held up by a circle of wooden posts. It is believed it may have had a reed thatched roof.

Britain's first semi-detached houses

The honour may go to what would now be called semi-detached houses, built at Arnford, near Long Preston, North Yorkshire, around 1690. London's first semis did not appear until some twenty years later.

Britain's first open prison

The country's first open prison was opened in 1936 at New Hall, near Wakefield.

Britain's tallest freestanding structure

Emley Moor mast

The giant Emley Moor transmitting station towers over Kirklees, West Yorkshire. Its 1,084ft (330m) tall concrete tower, now a Grade II Listed building, is the tallest freestanding structure in the UK. It is also, at the time of writing, said to be the twenty-fourth tallest tower in the world.

Constructed to supply television broadcasts to the Yorkshire area, the current mast is the third to be built on the site. The second mast, which was one of the tallest man-made structures in the world at the time, collapsed in March 1969. It had been weakened by a combination of strong winds and the formation of heavy ice on the structure. Miraculously, no-one was injured.

The current structure is so tall that reaching the top involves a seven-minute journey by lift. Due to its elevated position high on the Pennines, it stands 1,949ft (594m) above sea level.

England's longest place-name

At the foot of Sutton Bank, North Yorkshire, lies the pretty village of Sutton-under-Whitestonecliffe. At twenty-seven letters long, it has the longest hyphenated place-name in England. The village's other claim to fame is that it was once the home of Yorkshire vet and author James Herriot (aka Alf Wight).

England's oldest state school

The East Riding's Beverley Grammar School, founded in 700AD, is the oldest state school in England. Its former pupils include Thomas Percy, a member of the group who planned the 1605 Gunpowder Plot.

Britain's tallest lime tree

Measuring 154ft (47m) in height, a tree at Duncombe Park, Helmsley, North Yorkshire, is the tallest lime tree in Britain.

World's tallest folly

The Wainhouse Tower, in Halifax, West Yorkshire, is the tallest folly in the world at 275ft (84m) tall. Originally designed as a chimney, it was never used for that purpose, instead becoming an observatory. It was completed in 1875 at a cost of £14,000.

Britain's largest oak tree

The Cowthorpe Oak

The immense Cowthorpe Oak, in Cowthorpe, near Wetherby, West Yorkshire, was the largest in Britain. Its circumference had been measured at 60ft (18m), with its principal limb extending 48ft (15m) from the bole. The tree has sadly been rotting for many years. It was said to be decaying fast in 1822. Before its biggest branch fell in 1718, its branches were said to have "extended their shade over half an acre of ground; thus constituting, in a single tree, almost a wood itself".

The Lady's Slipper orchid, which was thought to have become extinct, still survives in Wharfedale

Britain's rarest flower

The Lady's Slipper orchid, which was thought to have become extinct towards the end of the First World War, still survives in Wharfedale, North Yorkshire. Its last native site is Grass Wood, managed by the Yorkshire Wildlife Trust.

Elisabeth Frink, Riace Figures, 1986–89

Britain's first sculpture park

Opened in 1977, the Yorkshire Sculpture Park, an open-air gallery in West Bretton near Wakefield, was the UK's first sculpture park. Its collection of works by Henry Moore is one of the largest open-air displays of his bronzes in Europe.

England's largest seabird colony

The coast between Flamborough Head and Filey, in the East Riding, is home to England's largest colony of seabirds. Each year more than 250,000 seabirds flock to Bempton Cliffs, which makes up part of this coastline. The cliffs are home to the only mainland gannetry in England and the largest kittiwake colony in mainland Britain.

World's most haunted city

According to a survey by the Ghost Research Foundation International, York is the most haunted city in the world, with a total of 504 recorded hauntings. The city's royal past, history of conflict and catalogue of notorious criminals is said to have resulted in a larger than average number of spooks and spirits. York is also said to be home to "the ghosts of greatest longevity", the Roman Legionnaires of the Treasurer's House (pictured below).

Oldest all-woman crew to row any ocean

The Yorkshire Rows

In 2016, four Yorkshirewomen became the oldest all-female crew to row across the Atlantic. The Yorkshire Rows team took under sixty-eight days to complete the 3,000-mile challenge. The women, all mums with children in the same school, were Niki Doeg, forty-five, Helen Butters, forty-five, Frances Davies, forty-seven, and Janette Benaddi, fifty-one.

During their epic adventure they faced everything from a hurricane to power failures and seasickness. They even had to row naked for a time after running out of clean clothes.

They took on the Atlantic Challenge to raise money for a Leeds cancer care centre.

After arriving back on dry land, Benaddi, the skipper, told the BBC: "Less than 100 women have rowed an ocean and now we as four mums have added to that and achieved a world record. What an incredible feeling to share as four best friends."

Left to right: Niki Doeg,
Helen Butters, Frances
Davies, Janette Benaddi

Britain's largest shellfish port

Bridlington, in the East Riding, has a historic reputation as a fishing port. This has been revived in recent years and it is now said to be Britain's largest shellfish port.

Britain's only full-time lifeboat crew

Established in 1810, the Humber Lifeboat Station at Spurn Point, in the East Riding, is the only RNLI lifeboat station with a full-time crew. The crews who have been based there during its long history have been awarded thirty-three medals for gallantry.

World's oldest surviving lifeboat

The *Zetland*, a lifeboat based in Redcar, North Yorkshire, was launched in 1802. It came out of service in 1864 after sustaining damage during a rescue and arrangements were made for it to be broken up. However, after anger among locals it was donated to the town providing it would not "compete" with the new lifeboat. Now its home is a free museum.

World's largest space hopper race

The unlikely record was broken in July 2010 at the Don Valley Grass Bowl in Sheffield. A total of 771 participants bounced their way to the record, raising £50,000 for local cancer charities in the process.

Establishment of the date for Easter

In 664AD a synod chaired by Abbess Hilda met at Whitby, North Yorkshire, to set the date for Easter celebrations. The church decreed that the Sunday on which Easter would be celebrated would be based on the phases of the moon.

Britain's first Christmas festival

It is said the first Christmas festival, "in the spirit of heathenish revelry, with feasting and mirth; in wantonness and many excesses", was celebrated by King Arthur in York in 521AD.

Britain's first turkey

The turkey was introduced to England by William Strickland of the East Riding of Yorkshire. He acquired six turkeys while on a voyage to America in 1526 and brought them back home. The drawing of his coat of arms is said to be the earliest depiction of the turkey in Europe.

World's most northerly wild hippopotamus

The furthest north the remains of a hippo have ever been found is in the Kirkland Cave, in the Vale of Pickering, North Yorkshire. The cave, discovered in 1821, contained the fossilised bones of hippopotamuses and elephants.

Britain's oldest bell

The country's oldest dated bell is housed in St James Church, Lissett, East Riding, and it dates from 1254.

Britain's strongest earthquake

Centred on a point sixty miles (97km) from the Yorkshire coast, the Dogger Bank earthquake of 1931 was the strongest ever recorded in the United Kingdom. Measuring 6.1 on the Richter scale, it caused damage in coastal towns, particularly in the East Riding.

Britain's oldest one-day agricultural show

Founded in 1796, Otley Agricultural Show has grown to become one of the most important shows in the north of England. It is believed a show of sorts was held in Otley, West Yorkshire, before the official foundation. Farmers held competitions for livestock classes at the Royal White Horse in Manor Square. Wharfedale Agricultural Society was formed in 1806 to formalise organisation of the event. The show was not held during the two world wars and it was also cancelled in 1983 due to waterlogging, but the event survived to celebrate its 200th anniversary in 1996.

World's longest-running horticultural show

The Ancient Society of York Florists claims to be both the oldest horticultural society in the world and also the organiser of the world's longest-running horticultural show. The society has held an annual show every year since its foundation in 1768, not even stopping during the world wars.

Britain's biggest maze

York Maze

Above:
Yorkshiremen
Geoffrey Boycott,
Jeremy Clarkson
and Brian Blessed
immortalised in the
York Maze

Created each year from more than one million maize plants, the York Maze is the largest maze in the UK. Each year's maze takes on a different theme, with the maize grown in recognisable shapes. In 2013, the world's biggest Dalek was created out of maize and a year later Brian Blessed was on hand to unveil a maze containing the faces of himself and fellow Yorkshiremen Geoffrey Boycott and Jeremy Clarkson.

World's most dangerous stretch of water

According to reports in the national press in 2016, the Strid, on the River Wharfe, North Yorkshire, could be the most dangerous stretch of water in the world.

England's shortest river

There are a number of challengers for the title, but the River Bain in North Yorkshire, a tributary of the River Ure, is believed to be England's shortest named river. The river is just two-and-a-half miles (4km) long, being fed by the natural lake Semerwater. At Bainbridge, where the river drops down a series of falls, the waters power a small hydroelectric project.

England's fastest-flowing river

The River Swale's name comes from the Anglo Saxon *Sualuae*, meaning rapid and liable to deluge. It is said to be the fastest-flowing river in England.

England's steepest public road

With a maximum gradient of 1 in 3, Rosedale Chimney Bank, North Yorkshire, is England's steepest road. A sign ominously warns drivers: "Dangerous hill. Engage low gear now. Cyclists please dismount."

World's largest samosa

The world's largest samosa weighed in at a whopping 244lb 4oz (110.8kg) and was created by a team at Bradford College in June 2012. The delicacy measured 53in (135cm) long, 33in (85cm) wide and 11in (29cm) high.

First person to appear on Channel 4

Richard Whiteley, from Bradford, was the first person to appear on Channel 4 when it was first broadcast in 1982. He was host of game show *Countdown*, which was recorded in Leeds.

Largest town in Britain not served by an A-road

It may be home to some of Britain's biggest brands, including Silentnight Beds, Rolls Royce and Esse stoves, but the West Riding town of Barnoldswick (now administered by Lancashire) is believed to be the largest town not served by an A-road. "Barlick" may be a little off the beaten track but it has a population of more than 11,000.

World's longest bunting

For more than a year residents of Cragg Vale beavered away, sewing 59,939 flags to stretch from the village of Mytholmroyd, West Yorkshire, all the way to the Lancashire border. The flags were linked to create a world-record-breaking seven-and-a-half mile (12.07km) length of bunting. The efforts were completed to mark the arrival of the Tour de France through Yorkshire in 2014.

The bunting was fashioned from curtains, tablecloths and even a butcher's apron. More than 280 locals took part. One woman, whose sister lives in the village, sent a length of flags from San Francisco and Dora Hirst, an eighty-five-year-old, single-handedly stitched more than a mile of bunting.

Longest-running sitcom in the world

Last of the Summer Wine

First broadcast as an episode of Comedy Playhouse on 4th January 1973, *Last of the Summer Wine* ran until 29th August 2010, making it Britain's longest-running comedy programme and the longest-running sitcom in the world. Filmed in and around Holmfirth, West Yorkshire (pictured below), every one of the 295 episodes was written by Yorkshireman Roy Clarke. In all, there were thirty-one series of what was said to be the Queen's favourite programme. There were also twenty-one Christmas specials, three television films, a documentary series, a television prequel, a number of novelisations and several stage adaptations. At its peak, in 1985, 18.8 million viewers tuned in.

Largest piece of fossilised human excrement

The Lloyds Bank Coprolite

This unusual record is thanks to a constipated Viking. It was dubbed the Lloyds Bank Turd – or, more politely, the Lloyds Bank Coprolite – after its discovery during a 1972 dig beneath the site of what was to become a branch of Lloyds TSB in York.

Measuring 8in (20cm) long by 2in (5cm) wide, it is believed to be the largest example of fossilised human faeces ever found.

Analysis of the stool suggested the producer lived on a diet of meat and bread, while the presence of hundreds of parasitic eggs suggested he was riddled with intestinal worms. York Archaeological Trust employee and paleoscatologist, Dr Andrew Jones, appraised the turd as "The most exciting piece of excrement I've ever seen. In its own way, it's as valuable as the Crown Jewels."

Unfortunately, in 2003, it broke into three pieces after being dropped. Commenting on its large size, conservator Gill Snape, who assisted in restoring the three pieces, remarked diplomatically: "Whoever passed it probably hadn't performed for a few days, shall we say."

England's oldest civic mace

The country's oldest civic mace that still survives is that of Hedon, in the East Riding. The silver-clad ceremonial mace, along with a charter, was presented in 1415 by Henry V. A mace was the weapon of the day and one would be carried by the mayor's sergeant to protect him as he went about his duties.

Most car lifts in an hour

Strongman Mark Anglesea of Whiston, near Rotherham, South Yorkshire, holds the record for the greatest number of times the rear of a car has been lifted clear of the ground. In 1998, at The Hind, Rotherham, he lifted a Rover Mini Metro 580 times in an hour.

The country's oldest civic mace is in the East Riding

World's longest charity live broadcast

The humanitarian charity PennyAppeal broadcast live from the British Muslim TV Studios in Wakefield between 2nd and 14th July 2015 – a record-breaking eleven days, eleven hours, eleven minutes.

Most radio DJs presenting one radio show simultaneously

BCB (Bradford Community Broadcasting), the community radio station for Bradford, broke the world record for the most DJs broadcasting on one show in March 2012. Sixty presenters took part, each introducing a song of their choice.

World's largest Indian restaurant

A stunning Grade II Listed Congregationalist chapel in Cleckheaton, West Yorkshire, was converted into an Indian restaurant in 2001. The result is now described as the largest Indian restaurant in the world. Aakash can seat 400 diners in the basement, 250 on the ground floor, and a further 200 on the horseshoe gallery.

World's longest group hug

A group of seven huggers spent twenty-five hours and ten seconds in a group hug to break this rather unusual world record. They achieved the feat at Leeds railway station between 19th and 20th September 2012. The huggers were Rachel Goodman, Emma Wilcock, Amanda Fothergill, Claire Kimberley, Dawn Matthews, Emily Boland and Jacqui Costello.

Britain's oldest chemist shop

Records show that medicines were first dispensed at Ye Oldest Chymist Shoppe in England in 1720. However, as the building itself, in Knaresborough, North Yorkshire, is 200 years older, it may have operated as a chemist shop from a much earlier date. It contained volumes of "dispensatories and herbals" from the seventeenth century. These days the shop sells Harrogate toffee and old-fashioned sweets. A blue plaque on the wall notes the shop ceased to be a pharmacy in 1997.

Seven people spent twenty-five hours and ten seconds in a group hug

World's oldest sweet shop

Although the sign above the door calls it the Oldest Sweet Shop in England, this quaint shop in the market town of Pateley Bridge, Nidderdale, North Yorkshire, has also been officially recognised by Guinness World Records as the longest continuously running sweet shop in the world.

Trading since 1827, the shop remained visually unchanged for 100 years. However, though it may appear as old-fashioned as its name would suggest, the sweet shop has not been afraid to move with the times, and for some years now it has also sold sweets online.

Britain's oldest independent co-operative store

Established in 1867, during the industrial boom, the Grosmont Co-operative Society Ltd, North Yorkshire, is the oldest independent retail cooperative in the UK. After 150 years it still supplies household essentials to the small Esk Valley community.

Britain's oldest farm shop

Founded in 1929, Hinchliffe's Farm Shop, Huddersfield, West Yorkshire, is Britain's first farm shop.

England's largest travelling fair

Hull Fair, which has been going for more than 700 years, now attracts more than half a million visitors during its annual week-long run. It is England's, and perhaps Europe's, largest travelling fair.

Britain's oldest pub

The Bingley Arms, Bardsey

The Bingley Arms, in Bardsey, north Leeds, is said to be the oldest in Britain. Once known as the Priest's Inn, its history can be traced back as far as 953AD when Samson Ellis brewed beer there. However, there is evidence to suggest there may have been a pub just a few yards away that was built in 950AD.

On the main route between Kirkstall Abbey and St Mary's, in York, it was a popular stop-off point for monks.

Inside the pub chimney are two priest holes dating back to 1538, where Catholic priests hid for safety during the Dissolution of the Monasteries.

In 1780 the pub was renamed after its owner Lord Bingley, taking the name by which it is known today.

In 2005, a book published by English Heritage cast doubt on the pub's alleged tenth-century origins.

Britain's highest pub

The Tan Hill Inn, Richmondshire

Standing at 1,732ft (582m) above sea level, in a remote corner of Richmondshire, North Yorkshire, the Tan Hill Inn is the highest inn in the British Isles. Pub-goers are often snowed in as the tavern's lofty position on the Pennine Way means severe weather is a common occurrence, and the publicans even have their own Snowcat for when conditions are at their most extreme. The cold climate resulted in the inn being chosen as the location for the filming of an advert starring Ted Moult for window-fitting company Everest. It also appeared on the first Vodafone commercial in the 1980s.

Although it now stands alone, the seventeenth-century building was once surrounded by miners' cottages, which were demolished in the '30s following the closure of the last mine in 1929. Never far away from the headlines, the inn has attracted a string of famous guests down the years and in 1995 it broke another record, becoming the first public house in the UK to be granted a licence to hold weddings and civil ceremonies following a law change.

World's largest glass of beer

Stod Fold Brewery

As the Tour de France passed through Yorkshire in 2014, Angus Wood, co-founder of the Stod Fold Brewing Company, Ogden, Halifax, West Yorkshire, poured a 3,664-pint (2082-litre) beer, a pint for every kilometre of the race. The giant glass was filled with local Stod Fold's Gold ale and was served up at The Fleece Countryside Inn, Ripponden, West Yorkshire.

UK's oldest publican

In August 2016, ITV *Calendar News* reported that eighty-seven-year-old Frank Collins was believed to be the oldest pub landlord in the country. Frank took over the running of the Dog and Partridge Inn, in Huddersfield, West Yorkshire, just before the death of his mother Mabel, who died in 2001 aged ninety-five. She had previously herself won a place in the *Guinness Book of World Records* for being Britain's oldest landlady.

World's biggest pie

For centuries Denby Dale, West Yorkshire, has been famous for pies. It is thought the first commemorative pie was baked to mark George III's return to sanity. Two hundred years later, in 1988, another mammoth Denby Dale pie broke the official world record. Serving more than 90,000 people, it weighed over nine tonnes, including 472.5 stone (3000kg) of beef, 472.5 stone (3000kg) of potatoes and 110 stone (700kg) of onions. At 20ft (6m) long, it was carved by more than 170 servers.

The Battle of Towton wiped out nearly one per cent of the English population

Britain's bloodiest battle

Almost certainly the bloodiest battle ever fought on British soil, the Battle of Towton (Towton being a small village near Selby, North Yorkshire) was so ferocious that nearly one per cent of the English population was wiped out in a single day. Between 50,000 and 80,000 soldiers took part in the 1461 battle between the Houses of York and Lancaster. It is reckoned 28,000 men lost their lives.

Greatest number of quilled flowers in one place

In September 2016 the Quilling Guild produced a record-breaking display of 6,241 paper filigree flowers. The flowers were on display at New Earswick Folk Hall, York.

World's oldest ever goldfish

The world's oldest captive goldfish died peacefully in his bowl in 1999 an incredible forty-three years after he was won as a prize at a funfair at Doncaster, South Yorkshire, in 1956. Tish was won along with another goldfish, Tosh, which died in 1975, as the prize in a roll-a-penny game.

Tish, owned by Hilda Hand, of Thirsk, North Yorkshire, turned from gold to a distinguished silver in old age. Hilda said Tish had "become something of a celebrity".

World's largest mosaic of sweets

Constructed over two days in February 2006, a mosaic made from sweets in Halifax, West Yorkshire, measured 33.6ft^2 (37.1m^2), at the time breaking the official world record. Sadly, the record set by Calderdale's education service has since been broken.

Thirty-two dames gathered outside York Minster

Most panto dames gathered in one place

In 2008, thirty-two pantomime dames congregated outside York Minster in a gathering organised by York Theatre Royal. It was claimed as a record on the basis that nobody else had ever attempted the feat.

World's smallest public art gallery

The Upper Settle phone box was purchased from BT by the local community of Settle, North Yorkshire, in early 2009. A use was required for the then-redundant red K6 box. It was decided to set up a community art gallery inside the kiosk, the Gallery on the Green. According to the gallery website, "We believe the Gallery on the Green is the smallest public art gallery in the world. Certainly it is the only one to be open 24/7 and filled to capacity at least twice a day."

World's biggest pantomime producer

Qdos Entertainment, of Scarborough, North Yorkshire, is the world's largest producer of pantomimes, with almost 700 productions to its credit over more than three decades. Its pantomimes are seen by more than two million people each year and a cast of 700 actors, dancers, musicians, stage staff and others work on its pantos.

World's first straw hat

Isabel Denton, of Leeds, is said to have invented straw hats in the time of Charles I.

World's largest Whitby jet gemstone

Visitors to W Hamond, the jet shop in Whitby, North Yorkshire, can see for themselves the record-breaking Whitby Jet gemstone. It measures a staggering 21ft (6.4m) in length, and was estimated to be 180 million years in the making.

World's largest longsword dance display

An impressive 186 dancers from seven schools performed a traditional Yorkshire Longsword dance in September 2003 at Halifax, West Yorkshire.

World's smallest nightclub

Measuring a tiny 3ft (0.9m) by 5ft (1.5m), "Club 28" in Rotherham, South Yorkshire, has capacity for three people – or six "at a squeeze" – plus a DJ. The converted shed includes a sound system, two turntables, a dance floor and disco lighting. Created by Jenkins-Omar and Stephen Robson, the creation was opened at the Rotherham Carnival in 2016. Revellers, who enjoyed a mixture of chart music, plus contemporary and classic house, were charged an entry fee of 50p.

First Briton to climb the world's fourteen highest mountains

Alan Hinkes, born Northallerton, North Yorkshire, is the first British mountaineer to have climbed all fourteen mountains with elevations greater than 8,000 metres (26,246.7ft). Hinkes climbed the first, Shishapangma, in 1987 and conquered his final summit, Kangchenjunga, in 2005. For his efforts he was awarded the OBE.

Oldest person to visit both Poles

Dunkirk hero and former Green Howards major Will Lacy visited both Poles in his eighties. Lacy, of Hawkser, Whitby, North Yorkshire, reached the North Pole in April 1990, aged eighty-two, and the South Pole in December 1991, aged eighty-four.

Fastest time to make a litre of ice cream

Chemist Andrew Ross had to get a moo-ve on when he whipped up a tub of ice cream in a flash. Watched by hundreds of people at Cliffe House Farm in Dungworth, near Sheffield, he slashed the previous record with a time of 10.34 seconds. The twenty-five-year-old Sheffield University PhD student used liquid nitrogen and some rigorous mixing to make sure he licked the competition.

A record 403 Bradford City fans donned flat caps

Fastest time to arrange a deck of playing cards

The record time to arrange into order a deck of shuffled playing cards was achieved at Sheffield Castle College in May 2008. Zdenek Vradac completed the feat in 36.16 seconds.

Greatest number of flat caps at a single venue

A record-breaking 403 Bradford City supporters donned flat caps at Valley Parade in April 2015. The unusual achievement was part of a fundraising campaign for Bradford's burns unit. The cost of buying a flat cap went to the good cause, and more than £10,000 was raised.

England's highest parish church

At approximately 1,400ft (426m) above sea level, St Mary's, Greenhow Hill, Nidderdale, North Yorkshire, is reputedly the highest in England.

England's largest parish church

Holy Trinity Church, Hull, is the largest parish church in England by floor area. Dating back to around 1300, the church is as old as the city itself. It was divided during the English Civil War, bombed in the First World War and spared during the Hull blitz of the Second World War. The church was granted Minster status in May 2017.

England's oldest Roman Catholic church

St Leonard and St Mary in Malton, North Yorkshire, has stood for more than 800 years. Founded in 1190, it is probably the oldest Roman Catholic church still in use in England.

England's largest churchyard

St Andrew's in Aysgarth, Wensleydale, North Yorkshire, is reputed to have the largest churchyard in England.

The Catholic church in Malton was founded in 1190

First woman to conduct a marriage ceremony in the Church of England

In March 1987, Reverend Sylvia Mutch became the first woman to conduct a marriage ceremony in the Church of England. The service at St Philip and St James's Church at Clifton, York, saw the wedding of Alastair Dearnley and Heather Irvine. Three camera crews and twenty three journalists were present. Yorkshire Television broadcast the wedding live.

Largest Gothic cathedral in northern Europe

York Minster measures 524ft (160m) in length and 249ft (76m) in height. Its nave is said to be the widest of any medieval cathedral in Europe. It is also home to the largest collection of medieval glass in the country.

Earliest English translation of the Bible

Yorkshire-born John Wycliffe produced the first English language Bible manuscripts back in the 1380s. In 1535, fellow Yorkshire-man Myles Coverdale, of Richmondshire, North Yorkshire, produced the first complete printed translation of the Bible into English.

England's oldest living convent

The Bar Convent, in York, was founded in 1686 as a school for girls. It is still home to members of the Congregation of Jesus today.

England's longest church clock pendulum

St Andrew's Church, Aldborough, near Boroughbridge, North Yorkshire, is said to be home to England's longest church clock pendulum. It measures 30ft (9.1m) long, with a swing lasting 3.4 seconds.

Europe's largest monastic ruin

Fountains Abbey, North Yorkshire, is said to be the largest ruined Cistercian monastery in Europe. It is also one of the best preserved.

Britain's largest stained-glass window

In the 1990s, Queen Victoria Street, in Leeds, was roofed beneath a vast expanse of stained glass, the largest stained-glass window in Britain.

Oldest surviving glass in England

The oldest extant glass in England is reputed to be a section of stained glass in York Minster dating from 1150, which is said to show a king entwined in the branches of a Jesse tree.

Most ushers to one groom and most bridesmaids to one bride

When Leeds couple Alexander Simmons and Amy Ewing married in February 2015 it was a really, really big day. They smashed two world records by having 136 bridesmaids and 97 ushers. To achieve the official Guinness World Records, the couple had to know all their attendants and couldn't just have random guests. The wedding, at Rudding Park Hotel, Harrogate, North Yorkshire, cost the couple nothing as they won a competition run by bridal shop owner Abbi Lewis, who wanted to create a record-breaking wedding.

Yorkshire-born John Wycliffe produced the first Bible in English

World's largest mascot race

Each year, dozens of giant animals, characters and other mascots gather at Wetherby Racecourse, West Yorkshire, to race and raise funds for Sue Ryder. The world record was broken in 2015 when 125 participants took part.

World's biggest collection of Daleks

Rob Hull of Doncaster, South Yorkshire, has been collecting model Daleks for years. At the last count he owned more than 1,800, and the number is growing all the time. Remarkably, Rob says he's "never been a fan" of *Doctor Who*, but he has been fascinated by the Doctor's arch enemy since he first saw one in a toy shop as a child.

World's heaviest gooseberry

In 2009, seventy-three-year-old Bryan Nellist, of Whitby, North Yorkshire, grew the world's biggest gooseberry, which weighed in at a whopping 2.19oz (62.01g). The bumper berry was unveiled at the annual Egton Bridge Gooseberry Show, the country's oldest gooseberry show. Bryan beat the previous record, held since 1993 by Cheshire's Kelvin Archer. He said: "Kelvin is the Cristiano Ronaldo of the gooseberry world and it is an honour to beat him". Kelvin later won back his place in the *Guinness Book of World Records* with a 2013-grown gooseberry weighing in at 2.27oz (64.49g).

World's biggest Yorkshire pudding

In 1996, the Yorkshire pudding found its way into the record books when members of the Skipton Round Table at Broughton Hall, North Yorkshire, made a pudding with an area of 500ft^2 (46.4m^2).

World's biggest drystone wall maze

The brainchild of North York Moors waller Mark Ellis, it is hoped the world's largest drystone wall maze, at Dalby Forest, North Yorkshire, will be opened to the public some time in 2019, subject to funding and weather conditions. The wall will be built from more than 4,000 tonnes of suitable stone.

Fastest time to pack a suitcase

A holidaymaker at the Primrose Valley Holiday Park, Filey, North Yorkshire, broke the record for the fastest packing of a suitcase in the summer of 2016. Rosie Marshalle packed twenty items in 46.18 seconds.

World's biggest beach angling festival

The Paul Roggeman European Open Beach Championship, held every year on the East Riding coast, attracts an estimated 1,000 anglers, each hoping to reel in a share of £35,000 in prize funds.

World's first professional wildlife photographers

Richard and Cherry Kearton (pictured right), from Thwaite, North Yorkshire, were probably the first professional wildlife photographers in the world. Cherry took the first-ever photograph of a bird's nest containing eggs in 1892.

Picture credits